HAYES TECHNOLOGY SERIES

FLIGHT

WRITTEN BY: DAN MACKIE
ILLUSTRATED BY: STEVE SHULIST
ART DIRECTOR: MARK HUGHES

©1986 Hayes Publishing Ltd., Burlington, Ontario

ISBN 0-88625-112-5

Hayes Publishing Ltd. 3312 Mainway Burlington, Ontario L7M 1A7

U.S. NAVY BLUE ANGELS

ACKNOWLEDGEMENTS

As an aviation enthusiast and pilot, I have read and written for most of the major aviation journals in North America at one time or another, and I belong to or have been associated with many clubs and organizations over the years. By far the most influential force in my own personal development of flying has come through my connections with the Experimental Aircraft Association with headquarters at Wittman Field in Oshkosh, Wisconsin. EAA is an international organization that fosters building your own airplanes. Without them, I would not have had the pleasure of building and flying a little biplane like the one on the cover of this book. Nor would I have had so much information on flying at my disposal.

ON THE COVER:

The Eagles Aerobatic Team, flying a formation aerobatic routine over Wittman Field.

CONTENTS

C.A.F. SNOWBIRD

ABOUT THIS BOOK

Have you ever dreamed about flying by yourself? Many people do, you know. They dream that if they flap their arms hard enough they can fly, or maybe if they wiggle their feet like a fish, they will rush into the air. Other people simply watch the birds, and wish -- wish that they could soar alongside them, feeling free and able to will their way over the hills and fields. Still others are terrified of heights, preferring to leave it to the birds! How unlucky they are!

Wanting to fly like a bird has been with man forever. It is the pleasure of it -- the dreams-- that made him first want to fly, and, no doubt, that was what led him to actually do it. Once he learned to fly, he began to find uses for it -- first as a sport, then for observing things, then for war, for travel and exploration, until finally many of us think of airplanes as a necessity of life. We use them to visit relatives and friends just as easily as riding a bus. And how many businessmen need to travel across the country in a plane for a meeting today?

But flying for pleasure and sport is still very much with us today. There are far more light planes flying than there are airliners. Hang gliding, ballooning, skydiving, ultralight flying, aerobatics and just plain flying for pleasure are continuing to satisfy the dreams of enthusiasts all over the world. And we certainly should not fail to mention the millions of model airplane builders and flyers - from paper airplanes to highly sophisticated radio-controlled models. It is a very serious and pleasurable way to enjoy the mysteries of flight.

This book is meant to give you an overlook of many sides of flight, some of which may be new to you. We are sure that if you dream of flying, a little bit of your dream will come true on these pages, for flight is one of the most exciting things in the world. One more thing, if what you see and read in this book is exciting to you, you can be sure that it is only the beginning in satisfying your dreams of flying, because flying is like music -- the more you like it, the more of it there is to like!

BIRDS

Initially, birds inspired us to fly, but they became more than just inspiration — they became models for us to copy. Why couldn't we just flap our arms and take off like a bird?

The first thing that comes to mind is that birds have wings and we don't. So why don't we just strap some wings onto our arms and flap off? Well, some men have tried that, but they found that they just couldn't flap hard enough, and, if they tried to glide from a high place, they weren't strong enough to hold their arms out.

HUMMINGBIRD

If you study the birds, you will find that they are much lighter for their size than we are. They have hollow bones, and their feathers have lots of air spaces in them and are extremely strong. Then if we look a little further at their heart muscles, we find that they are much stronger than we are for their size.

HERRING GULL

Even birds have some problems, though, and are constructed differently for different situations. Birds that fly over water for long periods of time, such as gulls, and birds that soar over land, such as hawks, have long narrow wings that are very large for their bodies. They don't flap their wings too much, but soar on updrafts of air. Birds that spend a lot of time on the ground, like chickens, have stubby wings and are poor fliers. Some birds, like the ostrich, have lost the ability to fly altogether, but have developed the ability to run very fast instead.

Then there are birds like the hummingbird that have short wings, but can flap them at very high speeds, allowing them to hover like a helicopter.

Penguins can neither fly nor walk very well, preferring to slide on their bellies and swim.

Man has been trying to fly by his own power for years without too much success. Finally, in 1977, a designer named Paul Macready won the Kremer prize for manpowered flight, and later, his plane flew across the English Channel. In both cases an extremely light aircraft had to be built with large, long wings. It was so light, in fact, that a strong gust of wind could tear it apart. And the pilot had to work so hard at pedaling it like a bicycle that he very nearly did not make it!

THE GOSSAMER ALBATROSS

HOW DO BIRDS FLY?

A bird's wing, if you could cut through it and look at a section of it, is curved as shown in the diagram. If we imagine the air passing over the wing instead of the wing passing through the air, and if we could see the air as lines or streams, we would see that the air passing over the top has to travel farther than the air passing underneath. (Tests have

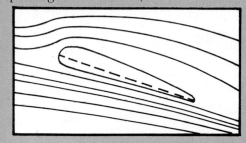

shown that the effect is the same.) If the airstreams before the wing are to meet at the end of the wing, then the air on top has to stretch to cover the extra distance. We know that air consists of tiny particles (molecules) and that the more molecules in a given volume, the higher the pressure. So, if you have to stretch the air, then there have to be fewer molecules in it. If it has fewer molecules in it, then the pressure is lower. If that happens, it means that there is higher pressure on the underside of the wing than on top, and so the air pushes upwards, and the wing flies!

You can prove that to yourself by sticking a piece of paper on a pencil as shown in the diagram. If you blow on the top, the paper will rise!

But that's only half the story. If you are riding in a car and you stick your hand out the window (carefully!), you can feel the air trying to lift your arm if you just tilt it a little. That's because the air striking your hand is deflected downwards. The reaction to this is to push upwards, but it also causes the air over top of your hand to curve.

So, lift is caused in two ways -- by the shape of the wing and by the angle at which it meets the air. The shape of the wing is called an airfoil. The angle at which it meets the air is called the angle of attack.

Airplanes have airfoils that are specially designed for the type of aircraft. You can make a glider that has no airfoil, just a flat wing. It will still fly, using the angle of attack, but a curved airfoil would be much more efficient.

DIVING   LANDING   TURNING

HOW DO BIRDS STEER?

Birds can climb by flapping harder or by riding updrafts of air. They dive by making their wings smaller. Hawks and Kingfishers, for example, tuck their wings in closer to their bodies to dive. When birds want to land, they hang their tails downwards to catch air and increase their angle

of attack, flapping to control their rate of fall.

When birds want to turn, they can do it by adjusting their wing feathers. Spreading them on one side increases the area and lift on the side, so that they bank. They can also bank by twisting one wing a bit (increasing its

angle of attack and, therefore, its lift). Once they are banked, the lift of their wings is at the angle and they begin to turn by tilting their tails and by hanging their tail feathers down on one side, which catches more wind on one side than the other.

HOW ARE AIRPLANES STEERED?

Airplanes use a rudder and elevators on the tail and ailerons on the wings for steering. The rudder is used to make the airplane yaw. The elevators make the plane pitch up or down. The ailerons make the airplane bank by changing the shape of the airfoil, which also deflects air upwards and downwards. (One side goes up, while the other side goes down.)

LEGENDS AND FABLES

ICARUS

A Greek myth tells us of the first notions of man flying. Daedalus made wings of bird feathers held together with wax so that he could fly across the sea with his son, Icarus. Daedalus warned Icarus not to fly too high, but Icarus was so enthralled with flying that he did not listen to his father. He flew too close to the sun, which melted the wax on his wings. They came apart, and he fell to his death in the sea.

OTTO LILIENTHAL (1849-96)

A mechanical engineer, living in Berlin, Germany, Otto Lilienthal became the first man to make controlled flights. Lilienthal built an artificial hill to try his hang glider designs. It was shaped like a volcano so that he could fly in

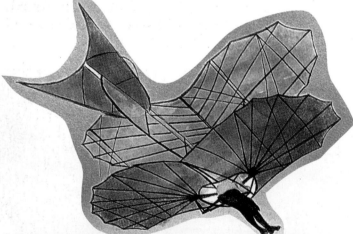

any direction. Inside the top was a hangar for storing gliders.

Lilienthal built monoplane and biplane gliders. They were hang gliders -- the pilot was supported by putting his arms through a yoke. The gliders did not have any controls. Lilienthal shifted his weight to make the gliders bank or

LEONARDO DA VINCI

A famous painter, inventor and genius, born in Italy in 1452, da Vinci is best known for his paintings The Last Supper and The Mona Lisa. Leonardo da Vinci experimented with many inventions, including flight. He designed the first helicopter and an ornithopter, which is an airplane that flies by flapping its wings.

One glider design that he had built so excited his assistant that he tried it while da Vinci was away. He crashed and killed himself. This so

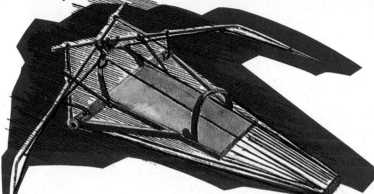

depressed da Vinci that he destroyed all of his designs and gave up experimenting with flight forever. Otherwise we may have manned flight 400 years earlier.

pitch up or down, swinging his legs forward to dive and backwards to slow down, and from side to side to keep it level or to turn.

Over 1,000 flights were made from his artificial hill before Lilienthal crashed and killed himself in 1896. He died while flying from the hills at Gollenberg in one of his monoplanes. Although it was a clear and sunny day, severe gusting conditions led to his crash.

OCTAVE CHANUTE (1832-1910)

An American civil engineer, Octave Chanute, retired in 1899 to study gliding. After studying Otto Lilienthal's work, Chanute incorporated Australia's Lawrence Hargrave's box-kite design into a successful hang glider. Its principles became the basis for work by the Wright brothers.

THE WRIGHT BROTHERS

Wilbur (1867-1912) and Orville (1871-1948) Wright were self-made engineers who designed and built bicycles in Dayton, Ohio. They became interested in the works of Lilienthal and Chanute in 1899 and began experimenting with gliders. By studying the way buzzards flew, they came up with the idea of twisting the wings for roll control. Wing-warping was tried on kites and later on a glider. In 1902, the Wrights made over 1,000 flights in a glider, which proved their methods of control that included a rudder, elevator and wing-warping.

Among the things that they learned were that if you simply rolled a glider, it would turn, but it would also sideslip towards the lowered wing. A glider would also turn just with rudder, but it would skid. The Wrights learned that if both rudder and wingwarp were used,

then a smooth turn would result with neither sideslipping nor skidding.

The Wright brothers were intent on powered flight. They figured out that thrust could be made by a propeller, which works like two wings rotating. The "lift" then becomes thrust. Most engines available in those days were too heavy, so the Wright brothers built their own. It produced about 12 horsepower, driving two propellers through chains.

The Wrights decided to test their machine at the Kill Devil Hills in North Carolina, where winds were steady and there was a lot of soft sand on which to land. On December 17, 1903, they made their first flight, which lasted 12 seconds and covered 120 feet. Their fourth flight of the day lasted 59 seconds and covered 852 feet. Powered flight had arrived!

GLEN CURTISS (1878-1930)

Chief rival of the Wright brothers was Glen Curtiss, who adopted the use of ailerons after an idea created by Robert Esnault-Pelterie of France. Curtiss' main talents lay in engine design. He displayed a fine airplane at the Reims airshow in 1909, called the Golden Flyer.

HANG GLIDERS

Hang gliding lay dormant for over fifty years after Otto Lilienthal and Octave Chanute made their experiments. Dr. Francis Rogallo made a breakthrough in the late 1940's when he began experimenting with models. The result was the Rogallo Wing, which consisted of three equal-length tubes and a tubular spar, supporting a flexible triangular sail. The idea was developed during the early days of the NASA space program as a maneuverable re-entry parachute, but the idea was dropped with the success of water landings.

In 1963, three Australian waterskiers, Bill Bennett, John Dickenson and Bill Moyes, tried towing a Rogallo wing behind a boat. They discovered that the wing could be released and would glide in controlled flight by shifting their weight.

Meanwhile, hang gliding was being experimented with in Southern California by Volmer Jensen and Richard Miller, among others. Miller's designs were made of bamboo and plastic film. Parallel bars were suspended under the glider from which the pilot hung by his armpits -- a very insecure and uncomfortable position. He controlled the glider by shifting his weight.

Finally, the Americans and Australians got together in 1969 and their technology was combined. Most significant was the adaptation of a triangular control bar and a bosun's seat for the pilot.

While record flights were being made, the sport of hang gliding grew through the 1970's with many problems, and many deaths and injuries. Rogallo wings had one major flaw in the design, and that was that if the sail collapsed on one side, say from a downgust of air, the wing went into a spin from which there was no recovery. Naturally, the sport gained a reputation for being extremely dangerous. But designs improved -- the problem with the Rogallo concept was solved by adding battens and a reflex shape to the wing -- and training improved, so that the sport of hang gliding enjoys a safety record that is extremely good.

FLYING A HANG GLIDER

Learning to fly a hang glider requires about twenty hours of classroom work, a lot of study and about fifty supervised, short flights. Pilots have to learn aerodynamics, how to look after a glider, how to read the weather, flying techniques and safety.

THE LAUNCH

Launches can be more dangerous than landings. Often you will see pilots sitting at the top of the hill hooked into their glider, just waiting and studying the "telltale" -- a string hanging from their front wires. When conditions are right, he will stand, lift the glider and adjust the angle of attack of the glider by feeling how it responds to the wind. Then he will run like mad down the hill until the glider picks him off the ground.

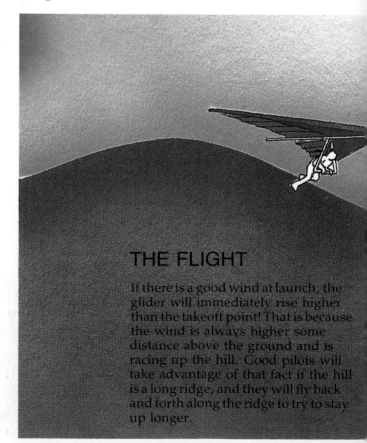

THE FLIGHT

If there is a good wind at launch, the glider will immediately rise higher than the takeoff point! That is because the wind is always higher some distance above the ground and is racing up the hill. Good pilots will take advantage of that fact if the hill is a long ridge, and they will fly back and forth along the ridge to try to stay up longer.

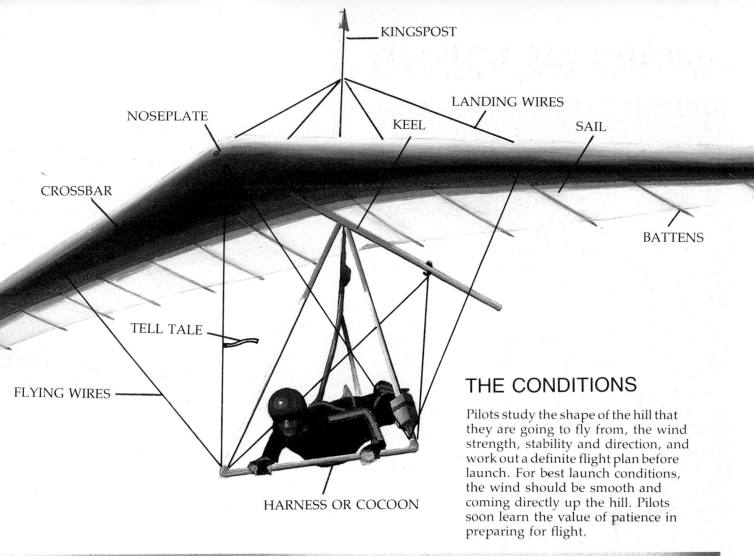

KINGSPOST

LANDING WIRES

NOSEPLATE

KEEL

SAIL

CROSSBAR

BATTENS

TELL TALE

FLYING WIRES

HARNESS OR COCOON

THE CONDITIONS

Pilots study the shape of the hill that they are going to fly from, the wind strength, stability and direction, and work out a definite flight plan before launch. For best launch conditions, the wind should be smooth and coming directly up the hill. Pilots soon learn the value of patience in preparing for flight.

THE LANDING

Pilots always try to land into the wind so that they don't have to run too fast. If they time it right, the pilot can skim along the ground, pushing the nose up gradually until the glider slows down, eventually stalling. If he can judge it right, the stall will occur just above the ground, and only a couple of steps will be needed.

To steer, the pilot shifts his weight around as he hangs inside the triangular control bar. If he pulls himself forward, the glider will speed up and dive. If he pushes the bar forward, the nose will push up and the glider will slow down. If he holds it up too high, the glider will stall. To turn, he shifts his weight from side to side.

If there are thermals (rising bubbles of hot air) around, the pilot will try to circle in them, rising like a gull or a buzzard. Flights of several hours have been made in this way, taking off from a modestly high hill! Also cross-country flights of over a hundred miles have been made by flying from thermal to thermal.

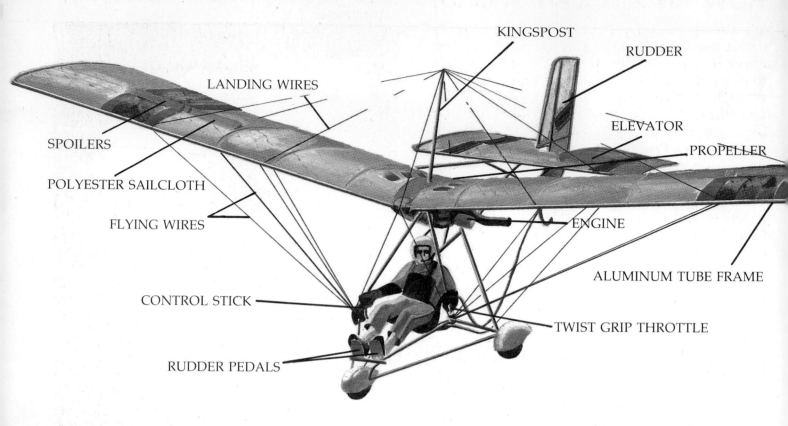

KINGSPOST
RUDDER
LANDING WIRES
SPOILERS
ELEVATOR
POLYESTER SAILCLOTH
PROPELLER
FLYING WIRES
ENGINE
ALUMINUM TUBE FRAME
CONTROL STICK
TWIST GRIP THROTTLE
RUDDER PEDALS

ULTRALIGHT AIRCRAFT

In Europe and Canada, ultralights are called microlights, but in the U.S.A. the common term is ultralight, which means a very light airplane with an engine.

Ultralights grew out of the hang gliding movement. The very first ultralight in the United States consisted of a hang glider, powered by a chainsaw engine that was mounted on the pilot's back! That was at the annual Otto Lilienthal meet in California in 1974. Pilots flew hang gliders off a hill towards the ocean. The fellow with the engine on his back had to go off the hill, too, because the engine did not provide enough power for takeoff. When he did get airborne with his engine running, he did not fly any farther than anyone else because the combination of hang glider and engine was so heavy. What was worse, he made an uncontrolled landing and wound up on his back, spinning around and around until some men carried him to the ocean where they dunked the engine in the water to get it to stop!

Original government requirements defined an ultralight as an airplane that could be foot-launched. Later, that got changed to limit the speed and weight, since most ultralights had

wheels and would never be foot-launched. Ultralights became very popular in the United States and Canada when the cost of private airplanes rose in the 1970's. Many manufacturers began making kits and selling ultralight airplanes that were based on hang glider designs. Over 20,000 of these were sold in just a couple of years. They were easy to fly compared to normal airplanes, and so a lot of people taught themselves to fly. Problems began when unscrupulous or incompetent manufacturers sold inadequately-designed aircraft to ill-trained customers. A lot of people died while flying ultralights. It was a similar situation that pioneers faced in the Wright brothers' time and later in the hang gliding movement.

As you read this book, men are debating whether or not governments should bring in strict rules to control the selling of ultralights and the training of pilots, or whether the manufacturers and pilots should get together to form their own rules. What do you think they should do? Certainly, governments should create rules to prevent people from hurting others, but should they have rules to prevent people from hurting themselves?

HOW AN AIRPLANE FLIES

We already talked about how a wing produces lift. It needs to be pushed through the air fast enough to make it lift, though. A glider needs to move through the air fast enough to produce enough lift to make it fly. If you take your glider and throw it gently, it will stall and dive to the floor -- not enough speed to make it fly. If you throw your glider very hard, it will zoom towards the ceiling before it runs out of speed and stalls -- too much speed! Too much lift! If you practice throwing it at just the right speed, it will glide smoothly to a landing. What is happening? The lift produced by its wing exactly balances the weight of the glider. If we call lift L and weight W, then $L = W$ for smooth flight.

If we wanted to have the airplane fly level, we would have to pull it through the air at just the right speed so that $L = W$. But what are we pulling against? It's just air, isn't it? So why do we have to pull it? If you stick your hand out of a car window (carefully!), doesn't air try to pull your hand backwards? We call the force of the air drag, and the pull necessary to overcome it is called thrust. So if we call drag D and thrust T, doesn't T have to equal D to sustain level flight? So, if we look at the diagram, we can see the forces that act on an airplane in level flight. In a glider, the T is provided by gravity.

When a pilot flies an airplane, he makes it go up or down by controlling the power of the engine. When he wants it to climb, he increases the power; when he wants it to glide or come down, he decreases the power.

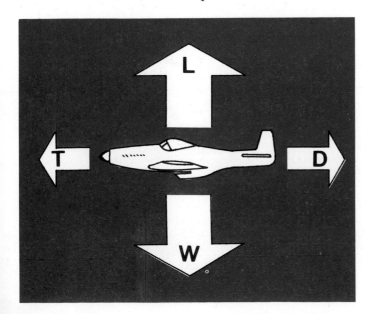

Make yourself a paper glider, following the instructions.

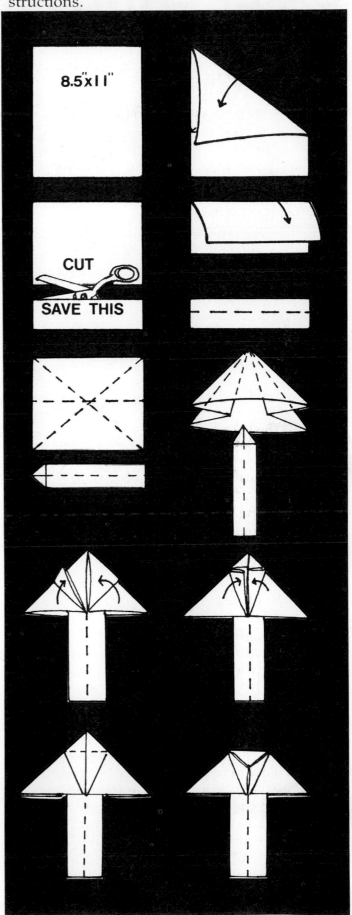

SAILPLANES

People who fly powerless planes rarely call it gliding, nor do they refer to their aircraft as gliders. Instead, the sport is known as soaring, and the aircraft are called sailplanes. This is because there is a lot more to soaring than just gliding from a high point to a low point.

In the past, however, there was gliding and there were gliders. Before World War II, a great number of German youth were trained in primary gliders, gliders and sailplanes in order to prepare them as pilots for the Luftwaffe or German Air Force.

To begin actual flight training, a primary glider was fixed on a pivot at the top of a hill, and when the wind was strong enough, a boy could sit on its seat and feel the effects of the wind on the controls.

Once the instructors felt that he was ready to try a flight and after he had had sufficient classroom training, a group of boys would hold the glider down, while another group would begin running down the hill, holding onto a tow rope that was attached to the glider. The tow rope had a bungee, or rubber section, in it which would stretch. At a given signal from the instructor, the boys holding the glider down would release it, and the glider would be catapulted into flight! Meanwhile, the instructor would run alongside with a megaphone, shouting instructions to the excited (and sometimes terrified) boy! There were many crashes, but the Luftwaffe produced thousands of excellent pilots.

Allied forces used gliders to land troops behind enemy lines.

LAUNCHING A SAILPLANE

Modern sailplanes are towed up behind airplanes. When the two aircraft are hooked together, two assistants are positioned at each wing of the sailplane to hold the wing up, because sailplanes only have one wheel to reduce drag. A launch director stands alongside the tow plane, waving his arm from side to side like a pendulum at which point the tow plane begins taking up the slack in the rope. As soon as the slack is taken up, the tow plane pilot applies full power. The two wing assistants run alongside the sailplane until the ailerons can hold the sailplane level.

THE TOW

The job of the tow plane pilot is to circle, gaining altitude, and to take the sailplane to an area of good lift upwind of the field. He has to keep his airspeed very low, because sailplanes fly slowly. The sailplane pilot's job is to stay exactly behind and slightly above the tail of the tow plane. The tow rope is released by the sailplane pilot at 2,000 feet above the ground. Immediately, the tow plane turns left and the sailplane turns right.

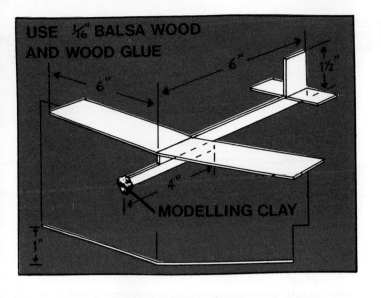

USE ⅟₁₆" BALSA WOOD AND WOOD GLUE

6"
6"
1½"
4"
MODELLING CLAY
1"

SPECIAL FEATURES ABOUT SAILPLANES

Sailplanes are built very light and strong. The first thing you will notice about them is that they are very sleek and have long, thin wings. What designers are trying to do is to minimize the drag, at the same time getting as much lift out of the wings as possible. By testing, engineers figured out that most of the drag on an airplane is caused by air that spins off the wingtips like two tornadoes. That is because the air on top of the wing is at lower pressure than the air underneath, and the high pressure air tries to sneak over the ends of the wings, and it comes off spinning like the dust cloud behind a car on a dirt road. These are called wingtip vortices. The narrow wings on a sailplane reduce the effect.

The other thing they found out is that the lower the span loading (in other words, the longer the wing) the higher the lift.

These two features give the best glide ratio, which means that the sailplane sinks very little for distance traveled.

THE FLIGHT

Sailplane pilots immediately look for lift after release. Most lift comes from thermals, which begin on the ground over a hot patch of land, beginning as a bubble of hot air, just like bubbles that are formed at the bottom of a pot of boiling water. Since hot air is lighter than cold air, the bubble of air rises, soon becoming a stream of rising air as the air underneath it is heated. Pilots look for likely places on the ground that would be hot, like a paved parking lot, a plowed field or large building. They also look for cloud "streets," or rows of puffy clouds (called cumulus clouds) that form at the top of thermals.

A pilot can feel the lift as a bump as he encounters a thermal, and he will feel the sailplane rising up like an elevator. Immediately, he will begin circling in an attempt to stay in the thermal. Some sailplanes have been lifted over 30,000 feet by thermals. By carefully flying from thermal to thermal, pilots can sometimes stay up for five or six hours.

THERMALS
— RISING AIR CURRENTS

THE LANDING

A pilot will think about landing at about 1,200 feet above the ground, making sure that he is close to the field and upwind. At about 800 feet above ground, he will fly parallel to his landing site, turning crosswind, then upwind to land. Most sailplanes use spoilers that come up on part of the wing to reduce lift and help them control their descent. Others use flaps and some even let out a little parachute to make drag and steepen their descent.

Once the wheel touches the ground, the pilot very soon rocks the sailplane forward onto its skid, which it uses as a brake. That is why most sailplane landing fields are grass. Rollout is very short, about 150 to 200 feet.

SPOILERS OUT

PRIVATE PLANES

CESSNA 172

Airplanes of every variety have been built for private use (two-seaters, four-seaters, six-seaters, single- and twin-engine, floatplanes) for a variety of purposes such as recreational flying, business flying, for farm use and many, many reasons. By far the most popular airplane for family use that was ever made was the Cessna 172. It was comfortable and easy to fly and could carry four people and their baggage.

WHAT IS A TAILSPIN?

If for some reason an airplane gets into a situation that one wing stalls but the other does not, then the nose of the airplane will pitch down and the plane will begin to spin. It will continue to spin until the pilot takes firm action to stop it. Engineers call tailspins autorotation, because the airplane will continue spinning by itself.

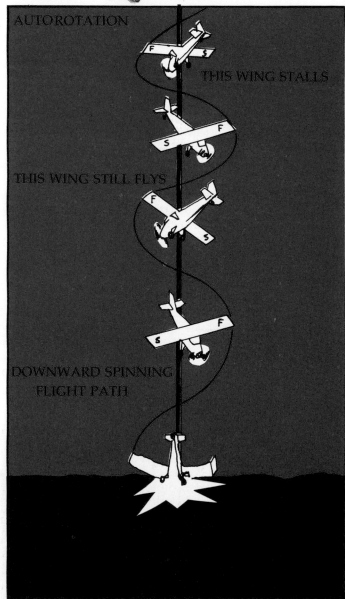

AUTOROTATION

THIS WING STALLS

THIS WING STILL FLYS

DOWNWARD SPINNING FLIGHT PATH

NOSE DROPS DOWN

FORWARD -INCREASED SPEED

BACK -DECREASED SPEED

ABRUPT YAW AT SLOW SPEED CAN CAUSE A SPIN

In the olden days, spins were feared, because airplanes spinned easily and pilots did not know how to recover. Airplanes of today are difficult to get into spins, but if you do, recovery can be instantaneous and simple.

BASIC CONTROLS

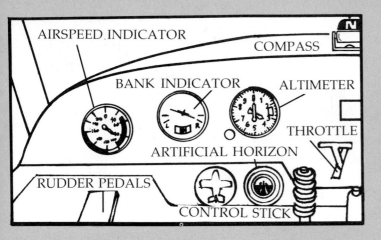

AIRSPEED INDICATOR
COMPASS
BANK INDICATOR   ALTIMETER
THROTTLE
ARTIFICIAL HORIZON
RUDDER PEDALS
CONTROL STICK

Most private airplanes have dual controls. This is because a pilot needs constant training throughout his life, and so he spends time with an instructor or check pilot. If he is a good, conscientious pilot, he will fly with an instructor at least one hour every six months. The reason for this is that people can develop bad habits without realizing it. It takes a second opinion, sometimes, to sharpen your skills. Even senior airline pilots have to take check rides.

Besides a control wheel or stick and rudder pedals, a pilot needs basic engine and flight instruments to fly. These are shown in the diagram.

HOW AN AIRPLANE ENGINE WORKS

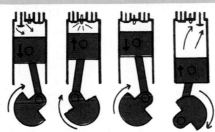

A gasoline-powered engine has a piston that rides up and down in a cylinder. The piston is connected to a crankshaft so that when the piston goes up or down, it turns the crankshaft, which is connected to the propeller. The top of the cylinder is blocked off, so that when the piston travels upwards, it squeezes the air inside. If gasoline is mixed with the air and just as the air is squeezed a spark is made inside the cylinder, and gas and air mixture will explode, driving the piston downwards, turning the crank and the propeller. The question is: How do we get the gasoline inside the cylinder?

Most gasoline engines have valves at the top of the cylinder that allow the air and gas into the cylinder, and also to let the smoke from the burned gas

(exhaust) out! This is usually done in four cycles: intake, compression, firing and exhaust, and so it is called a four-stroke engine. The four strokes are shown in the diagram:

Intake - The intake valve is open, and a mixture of gasoline and air is sucked in by the piston traveling downwards.

Compression - Intake valve is closed, piston travels upwards, squeezing the mixture of air and gas.

Power - A spark plug makes a spark and ignites the mixture. It explodes, driving the piston downwards.

Exhaust - The exhaust valve opens,

and the piston, which has leftover speed, travels upwards, pushing out the burned gases. The piston has so much momentum, in fact, that it continues around to the compression stroke.

After the internal combustion engine was invented, engineers found out that you could get more power and a smoother-running engine by having more than one cylinder. Most private planes have four- or six-cylinder engines.

Early airplane engines arranged the cylinders in a row or radially with some bigger engines having sixteen cylinders or more, sometimes arranged them in a V formation. Modern light planes have the cylinders horizontally opposed. Large piston-engined planes still use engines with cylinders that are arranged in a radial pattern, but they usually have rows of cylinders.

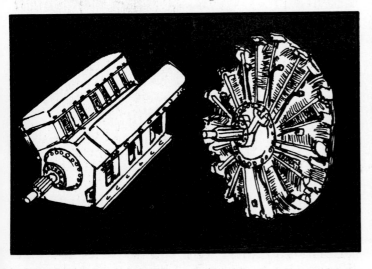

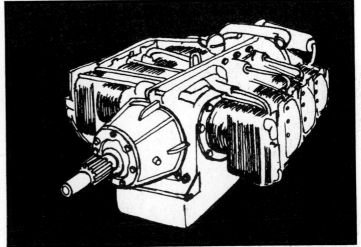

V-12 ENGINE   NINE CYLINDER RADIAL ENGINE   SIX CYLINDER HORIZONTALLY OPPOSED ENGINE

SPORT PLANES

EAGLE

ACRO ZENITH

DRAGONFLY

CANARD

COOT

People who are the most in love with flying fly sport planes. Most sport planes are homemade, but many are restored antiques. In either case, its owner is dedicated enough to put a great deal of effort into building, restoring and maintaining his airplane.

The Experimental Aircraft Association in Oshkosh, Wisconsin, is the center of sport aviation for the United States and all of the world. Each year it has a ten-day convention at Wittman Field, where some 500,000 people come to see some 10,000 airplanes. About 3,000 of the airplanes are home built. Others are antiques, warbirds, aerobatics airplanes, and ordinary factory-built private airplanes.

The nice thing about building your own airplane is that you can focus on exactly what you want from flying -- open cockpit, high speed, aerobatics, soaring, flying off water, or any combination of these things. There are many, many designs available, whereas there are only a few types of airplanes that are available from factories.

It takes a lot of hard work, but learning to build an airplane is as much fun as building a model aircraft, except that it takes quite a bit longer!

Some high schools have classes that build an airplane as a group project. EAA can provide manuals and plans and, on occasion, they help to find parts and equipment for the school. EAA was started by Col. Paul Poberezny in the basement of his home in Hales Corners, Wisconsin, in 1953. Since then, it has grown to have over 300,000 members worldwide. Building homebuilt airplanes has become so popular that there were more new homebuilts registered in 1984 than there were factory-built airplanes!

WOODEN AIRPLANES

MOSQUITO

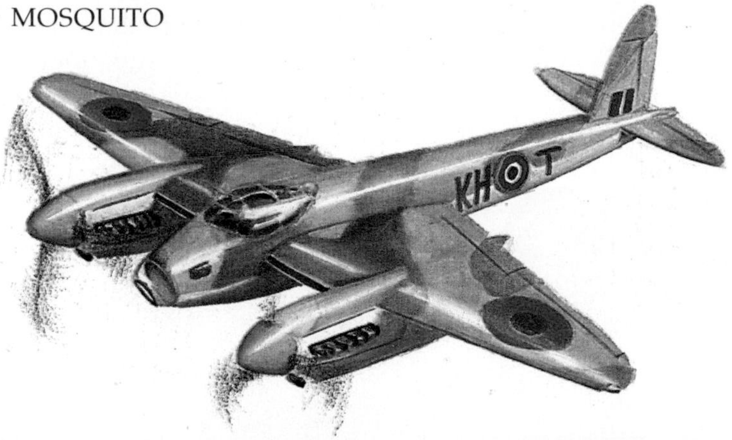

Almost an entire airplane can be made from wood. The best wood for making some parts of airplanes is Sitka Spruce, which comes from British Columbia and Alaska. Sitka Spruce comes from tall, straight trees. It is liked because it has a straight grain, is very strong and light, and does not split easily. Mahogany plywood is light and strong and comes from the Philippines and Honduras. The strongest plywood comes from Finland. It is made from birch trees. Resin glues are used to bond the wood together.

The fastest fighter in World War II (the deHavilland Mosquito) was made entirely from wood.

RAG AND TUBE

One of the best combinations for building airplanes is called "rag and tube" by aircraft lovers. Usually, this means that the fuselage, or body of the airplane, is built from steel tubing that is welded together, but the wings are made from wood. Both are covered with fabric.

POBER PIXIE

ALUMINUM

Most modern airplanes, from two-seat trainers to airliners, are made from aluminum. Aluminum is the least expensive method of building airplanes. Usually, the aluminum sheet is riveted together, but sometimes it is bonded with an epoxy glue. People who love "rag and tube" airplanes sometimes call aluminum airplanes "Spam cans," for fun.

SWEARINGEN SX300

COMPOSITES

Many modern airplanes are built from plastics, fiberglass and carbon fibers. Almost all high performance sailplanes, for example, are built from fiberglass. Sometimes polyurethane foam is used to carve out a desired shape and then it is covered with polyester cloth, which is then soaked in epoxy resin. Airplanes that are built combining wood, metal, foam, plastic, glass cloth, carbon fibers, etc. are usually called "composites."

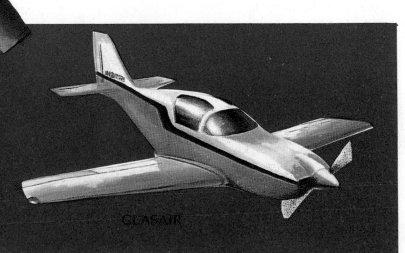

GLASAIR

AIR RACING

The very first air race was in Reims, France, in 1909, when Glenn Curtis won two prizes for speed at 46.6 and 47 mph in the Golden Flier. Then Bleriot won the 10-kilometer race at 48 mph.

In 1912 Jacques Schneider sponsored a seaplane competition by presenting the Aero Club de France with the now-famous Schneider Trophy. By 1931, the British won permanent possession of the trophy at an average speed around a course of 340.08 mph in the Super-

CONQUEST 1

AT-6

'RIVETS'

'STINGER'

RACING BIPLANES

THE RENO AIR RACES

Modern air races are typified by the annual event at Reno, Nevada, which is the biggest gathering of air racers anywhere. Four classes of races are held. These are the Biplanes, Formula l, AT-6 and Unlimited Classes. Biplanes are single-seaters with their engine size limited to about 125 hp. Formula 1 has no restriction, except that the engine size is limited to about 100 hp. AT-6's are ex-World War II

trainers, known as SNJ's by the Navy and Harvards by Canadians. Unlimited racers can be the most exciting class, but also the most dangerous, because engines are strained and sometimes they fail or even blow up! Most unlimited racers are highly modified WW II fighters. Biplanes and Formula 1 racers start from the ground. Men hold the tails of them, while the pilot revs up the

engine, then everybody goes when the starter waves a flag.
AT-6 and unlimited racers get a flying start. They go around the pylons, following a chase plane, usually a P-51 Mustang, flown by famous airshow pilot, Bob Hoover. When he is certain that they are all in proper formation, Bob Hoover calls them all on radio saying, "Gentlemen, you have a race!" Then he pulls up out of the formation, and the race is on!

marine S.6B. One of the racers from the 1929 race, which never completed the race, was the Italian Macci M-67. It set a seaplane speed record in 1934 at 440.7 mph which has not been beaten to this day!

In Cleveland, Ohio, the famous Thompson Trophy races began in 1929. Planes were flown around a course that was marked by pylons, which they had to clear to ensure that they covered the correct distance.

GEE BEE SUPER SPORTSTER

One of the strangest airplanes flown in the Thompson Trophy races was the Gee Bee. They were little more than a huge engine with stubby wings and were very difficult to fly. The Granville brothers built these. Seven were built and all crashed; however, not before Jimmy Doolittle set a landplane record of 296.287 mph in 1932.

The Thompson Trophy races ended in 1939, but picked up in 1949. One of the most famous racers, Steve Wittman, won the 1949, 1950 and 1952 Continental Trophy Races in his home-built Bonzo.

During the late 1930's, speed records for land-planes were being assaulted in Europe. By 1939, the world record was held by a German Messerschmitt Bf209, flown by Fritz Wendell at 481 mph. The Bf209 record stood until 1969, when an American, Darryl Greenamyer, flew his highly modified Grumman Bearcat, Conquest I, to beat the record by just one mph.

MITCHELL'S S.6B

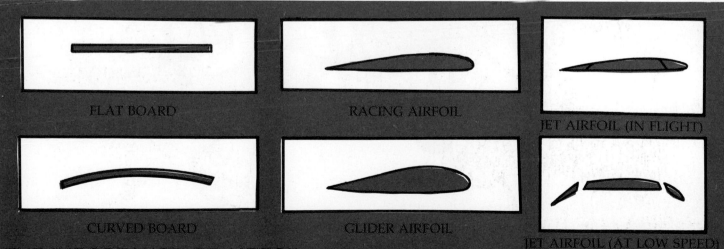

FLAT BOARD

RACING AIRFOIL

JET AIRFOIL (IN FLIGHT)

CURVED BOARD

GLIDER AIRFOIL

JET AIRFOIL (AT LOW SPEED)

THE IMPORTANCE OF AIRFOIL

Even a flat board can act as an airfoil, giving lift by its angle of attack, but it will stall sooner as the angle of attack is increased than would a flat board that has been warped into a curve. Also, engineers figured out that the higher the curve (up to a point) the more the lift, but also, the more the drag. Wouldn't it make sense, then, to make a racer with a

flatter airfoil than what you would make for a glider?

Racing planes have sharp-nosed, thin wings, but that also makes them difficult to fly, because they stall at high speeds, too. And a wing that is thin can flutter like a flag, so a design of wing has to be carefully done and tested so that this does not happen. Sailplanes have thick, curved wings.

These give high lift and stall at low speeds. When they do stall, it is a gentle stall, whereas a racing plane's stall will be very sudden and without warning.

Most high-speed planes have flaps and slats to change the shape of the wing so that they can land and take off more slowly and safely.

BIPLANES

WHY TWO WINGS INSTEAD OF ONE?

Man studied birds to learn how to fly, but he ignored some of the best creatures such as insects, some of which have two sets of wings. At first, it made sense to build an airplane with one set of wings. After all, if more than one set was better, why weren't birds built that way? It is quite likely that early experimenters found very quickly that long, thin wings couldn't be made very strong, but two shorter ones could. Sir George Cayley, known as the father of aeronautics, built a triplane glider in 1849, based on this idea. His coachman became the first man known to glide, but he promptly quit his job after the experience.

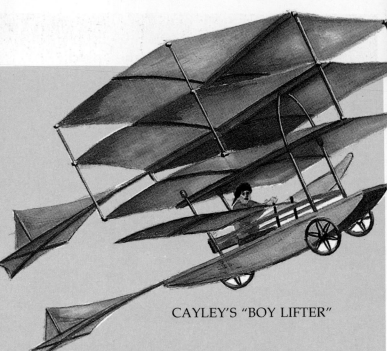

CAYLEY'S "BOY LIFTER"

this accidental way that the benefits of a thick airfoil were discovered. The new plane, the D-VII, was a terrific performer. Since the thick airfoil was so strong, Fokker followed the D-VII with the D-VIII, which was a monoplane. The future of the monoplane was assured.

FOKKER D-VII

Hargreave's box kite proved beyond doubt that double wings were stronger and, for the most part, aircraft developed around that idea. Most of the early World War I airplanes were biplanes. A couple of them, such as Manfred von Richtoven's "Red Baron," were triplanes. Anthony Fokker, a Dutchman who built airplanes for the Germans during World War I, was looking for a way to do without the wires that normally crisscross between the wings. In order to do that, he built a thick wing so that he could put a strong spar inside it. It was in

CAMEL F.1

HOW DOES A PILOT KNOW HOW HIGH HE IS FLYING?

A pilot reads his altitude on an instrument called an altimeter. It has three little hollow wafers inside that are sealed so that the air inside them cannot get out, just like tiny balloons. The higher an airplane goes, the lower the air pressure that surrounds it. Since the pressure inside the wafers is the same as it was on the ground, but everything around them has lower pressure as the plane climbs up, the wafers swell, like a balloon getting bigger. They push against little levers that operate gears that turn the hands on the altimeter.

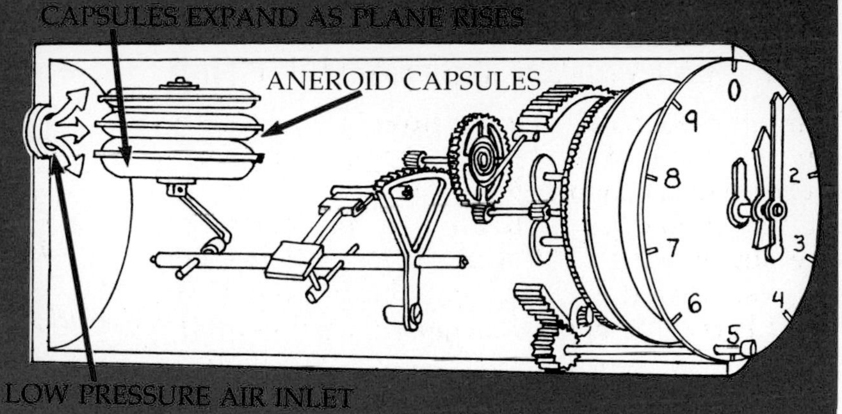

CAPSULES EXPAND AS PLANE RISES

ANEROID CAPSULES

LOW PRESSURE AIR INLET

GRUMMAN AG-CAT

PITTS SPECIAL

AN-2

MODERN BIPLANES

Although we think of biplanes as being old-fashioned, they are still being built and used today! The Russians use a very successful bi-plane for brush work. It is called the Antonov A-22. Crop dusting airplanes often have two sets of wings so that they can fly slowly, carry heavy loads and maneuver in tight turns close to the ground. Many aerobatics airplanes are biplanes. Besides being very strong, the wings can be kept short, which allows them to roll very fast.

AIR SHOWS

Air shows are demonstrations of aircraft and flying skills and can be as small as a grass strip community show to as large as the Paris Airshow. Sometimes they are called a Flying Circus.

The Paris Airshow is mostly a military and transportation display. It has a reputation as the most daring of shows, because aircraft manufacturers try to demonstrate maximum performance and constantly strive to outdo their competition. As a result, there are often come spectacular crashes.

Bob Hoover is one of the world's best air show pilots. He does a routine in a yellow P-5l Mustang that is exciting aerobatics. Then he does the unthinkable, shutting off the engine and performing an aerobatic routine as he glides to a landing, stopping within feet of his starting point! If you think that is spectacular, he then does the same routine in an ordinary, twin-engined executive plane, first with one engine shut down, then with both!

Another famous air show pilot is Art Scholl, who is a professor of aeronautics. He flies a

BOB HOOVER'S MUSTANG

LOUDENSLAGER'S LASER

FOUGA MAGISTER JETS
FRENCH AIR FORCE

modified deHavilland Chipmunk with colored smoke. Included in his spectacular routine is to pick up a ribbon stretched between two poles -- with his rudder while flying upside down!

One of the very best air shows in the United States takes place at the EAA annual convention at Oshkosh, Wisconsin, each August. The convention lasts for ten days and shows off more than three thousand homebuilt and specialty airplanes. In addition, there is an air show every day in the afternoon that features aerobatics, skydiving, warbirds, antiques, ultralights and sometimes a clown show.

Always a big part of large air shows are the military formation aerobatics routines. The Canadian Snowbirds and the U.S. Navy Blue Angels are two excellent examples.

Smaller airplanes are used in formation routines as well. The Eagles, biplanes flown by Tom Poberezny, Gene Soucy and Charley Hilliard, are an example. The French Connection, two CAP 10's, are also popular to watch.

AEROBATICS COMPETITIONS

BASIC MANEUVERS

All aerobatics maneuvers are combinations of looping, rolling, spinning and tumbling. Loops can be flown rightside up or upside down. A spin that is forced at any speed or direction is called a snap roll. (The British call it a flick roll.) A popular tumbling maneuver is known as a Lomcevak, which is a Czechoslovakian name that roughly means "headache."

COMPETITIONS

Four categories of competitions are designed for the level of skill of the pilot and the performance of his airplane. These are: Sportsman, Intermediate, Advanced and Unlimited. World competitions are in the Unlimited category only.

THE BOX

Pilots have to fly their aerobatics routines in a definite airspace known as "The Box," which is a cube that is 1,000 meters to the side. Markers on the ground are used to indicate the sides of the box.   To stray out of the box is to get penalty points.

THE AIRPLANES

Famous aerobatics airplanes include the Pitts Special, Lazer 200, CAP 21 (France), Zlin 50L (Czechoslovakia) and the YAK 55 (Russia).

FAMOUS CHAMPIONS

Victor Smolin (USSR), Leo Loudenslager (USA) and the 1984 Champion, Petr Jirmus (Czechoslovakia) are famous male champions. Women fliers from Russia have dominated their sport. Khalide Makagonova won in 1984. World championships are held every two years.

AEROBATIC AIRFOILS

Unique to aerobatic airplanes are their airfoils, which are equally curved on top and on bottom so that they will fly equally well upside down as rightside up. Airfoils are also thick for good strength and high lift. Sometimes the airfoil is different at the wingtip than near the fuselage so that the aircraft will spin better.

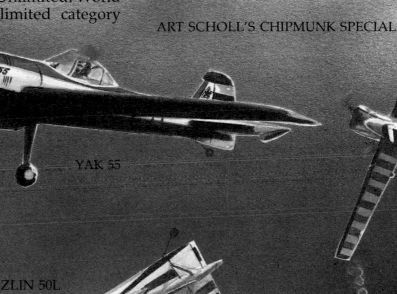

ART SCHOLL'S CHIPMUNK SPECIAL

YAK 55

ZLIN 50L

"g" FORCES

If you tie a weight on the end of a string and swing it around, the harder you swing it, the heavier the weight seems. This is called the centrifugal force. When the weight is at rest, it is said to have a mass of 1 g. If you swing it, so that it weighs twice as much, the force is said to be 2 g's.

A pilot flying a loop experiences about 3 g's. His arms will feel very heavy. Competition pilots can feel up to 6 or 7 g's. When that happens, the blood stops flowing to the brain, and the pilot can black out momentarily. When a pilot flies an upside down loop, the pressure of the blood in his head can cause him to "red" out. World competition pilots who fly a lot of upside down or "negative g" maneuvers usually have bloodshot eyes after flying.

SEAPLANES

Flying from water has been attractive since flying began, since the absence of smooth landing fields gave the seaplane more choices. This became particularly true for flying to remote places, such as the Arctic and the reaches of the British Empire in the early days.

FLYING BOATS

When the fuselage of the airplane becomes the hull or surface that contacts the water, the machine is called a flying boat.

FLOAT PLANES

A landplane that has pontoons attached to it is called a float plane.

AMPHIBIANS

Airplanes that have wheels that retract so that it can land or take off on either land or water are called amphibians. Float planes can be equipped with amphibious floats.

THE STEP

One of the difficulties in taking off from the water is to "unstick" the airplane. This is caused by the surface tension of the water and is directly related to the area of the plane that is contacting the water. You can demonstrate this to yourself in a swimming pool by using a styrofoam kickboard. If you hold the board on edge in the water, it is very easy to lift it out of the water, but if the board is lying flat in the water and you pull it straight out, it "sticks."

Pontoons and the hulls of flying boats have a step designed on their bottoms so that as the aircraft gains speed, it rides up on the step, thus reducing the surface area that is in contact with the water. Floatplane pilots who are flying a heavily loaded airplane on smooth water sometimes find that the plane is stubborn in "unsticking." Their solution to this is to bank the airplane, pulling one float out of the water at a time.

BUSH PLANES

Canada's Arctic was opened up by using float planes in the summer which they converted to ski planes in the winter. The Norduyn Norseman, built in Montreal, was a famous bush plane. Examples of modern bush planes are the deHavilland Beaver, Otter and Twin Otter.

WATER BOMBERS

World War II flying boats, such as the PBY, have been converted to use in fighting forest fires, because they can land on lakes and scoop up water to dump onto the fire. Canadair in Montreal builds the only modern water bomber at this time.

CANADAIR CL-215

NOORDUYN NORSEMAN

GRUMMAN GOOSE

FLYING BOATS

In 1914, the first passenger flying boat, the Benoist Flying Boat, operated between Tampa and St. Petersburg, Florida. It carried one pilot and one passenger, who was charged $5 for the trip, more if he weighed more than 200 pounds.

First airplane to cross the Atlantic Ocean was a Navy Curtiss NC-4 in 1919. It left Newfoundland and flew to the Azores, then on to Lisbon, and finally up to Plymouth, England, landing there fifteen days later with a crew of six.

In the 1920's, Imperial Airways of England began flying boat service to the British Empire Colonies, beginning with the 15-passenger Short S.8 Calcutta.

In the 1930's travel began with the famous China Clipper Flying Boats, built by the Martin company in the United States.

Shortly after World War II, grand plans were made for flying boat service. The Saunders-Roe Princess was one of the largest built in 1946. It had ten turboprop engines, each delivering 3,780 horsepower! It could carry 200 passengers at 360 mph.

The largest aircraft ever built was a flying boat, the Hercules, built by millionaire Howard Hughes. Construction began in 1942. First and only flight was in 1947, piloted by Howard Hughes, which took place over the harbor of Los Angeles and lasted only about a mile. The airplane had eight 3,000 hp engines. Its wingspan was 320 feet, or about the length of a football field. Designed as a freighter or troop transport, it could carry 700 passengers at 200 mph. Built entirely of wood, the flying boat got affectionately known as the "Spruce Goose," even though most of the wood used was Douglas Fir and birch plywood.

The Spruce Goose can be seen today in Los Angeles, where a special hangar was built for showing it to the public.

SUNDERLAND

SHORT S.8 CALCUTTA

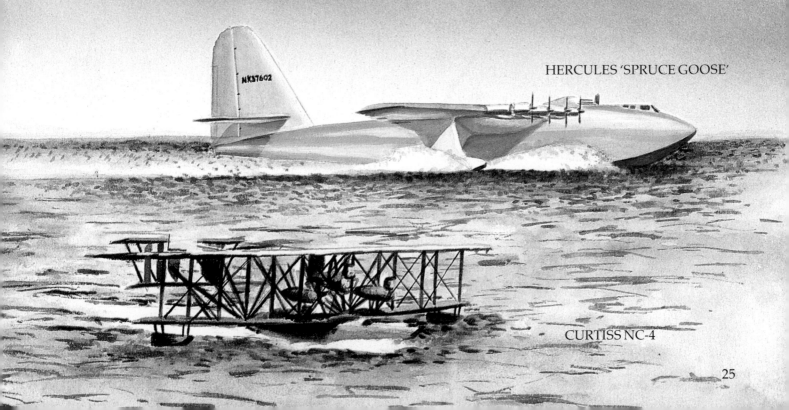

HERCULES 'SPRUCE GOOSE'

CURTISS NC-4

25

OLD WARPLANES

SOPWITH PUP

WORLD WAR I (1914-18)

The first world war began in 1914, barely five years after the Wright brothers demonstrated their Flyer in Europe. Aircraft were considered by the military as reconaissance and observation tools. Airmen began taking firearms along on their scouting flights, sometimes shooting a pistol at an enemy aircraft, and sometimes dropping objects on enemy troops below. Early experiments at mounting a machine gun on an airplane brought disastrous results. Sometimes, a distracted gunner would hit his own airplane!

On April Fool's Day in 1915, a French pilot, Roland Garros, mounted a machine gun on the fuselage of his Moraine-Saulnier Type L monoplane, pointing it through the propeller. He fixed steel wedges on the propeller to deflect any bullets that might hit it. On his observation flight that day, he shot down a two-seater Albatross, introducing aerial combat to the war.

The Germans soon developed an interrupter which used the propeller itself to fire the gun, preventing bullets from hitting the blades. Quickly, the Germans dominated the air war. The British tried other airplane designs, such as using a pusher propeller, and mounting the Lewis machine gun high on the wing, but these were not successful. Later, they developed a synchronized machine gun for the Camels and Scouts, and then began to regain control of the air.

BOMBING

Early dropping of objects on the trenches probably included anything heavy, such as bricks and stones, and it has been known that sacks of nails have been emptied onto the unsuspecting soldiers below. Hand grenades and special bombs meant to be dropped by hand were used.

Bombing was taken seriously during World War I. By the end of the war in 1918, just four years later, huge bombers with 100-foot wingspans were capable of dropping up to 2,000 pounds of bombs. The largest bombers were the Russian Ilya Mourometz, of which 73 were built. The largest bomb dropped was 1,650 pounds from a British Handley-Page 0/400.

FAMOUS FIGHTERS

MESSERSCHMITT ME109

ZERO

SPITFIRE

WORLD WAR II (1939-45)

Events leading up to World War II, such as Hitler's rise to power and the Spanish Civil War in 1936, helped to develop the airplane to the point that they were very fast and deadly by the start of the war. Still, the number and variety of aircraft and their advances over six short years are incredible. At the beginning of the war, both sides used biplanes as trainers: the Germans, the Buecker Jungmann, the British, the Tiger Moth, and the Americans, the Stearman. Yet, all had developed jets by the end of the war (including the Japanese).

Many museums throughout the world have WW I and II aircraft on display. These include the Shuttleworth Collection in England, The Smithsonian in Washington, D.C., and The National Aeronautical Museum in Ottawa. Two organizations that maintain a flying collection are The Canadian Warplane Heritage in Hamilton, Ontario, and the Confederate Air Force in the United States. These two organizations participate in many air shows in North America during the summer months.

CORSAIR

LANCASTER

JET PLANES

First jet engines were built and tested almost at the same time in 1937. In Germany, Pabst von Ohain designed one, while in England, Frank Whittle was the designer.

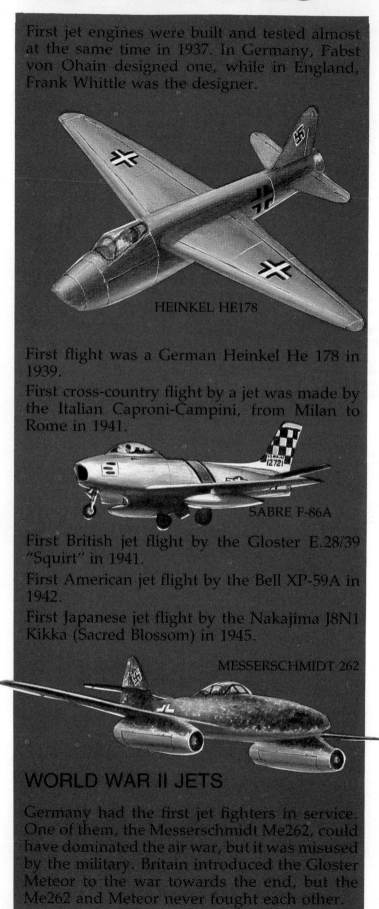

HEINKEL HE178

First flight was a German Heinkel He 178 in 1939.

First cross-country flight by a jet was made by the Italian Caproni-Campini, from Milan to Rome in 1941.

SABRE F-86A

First British jet flight by the Gloster E.28/39 "Squirt" in 1941.

First American jet flight by the Bell XP-59A in 1942.

First Japanese jet flight by the Nakajima J8N1 Kikka (Sacred Blossom) in 1945.

MESSERSCHMIDT 262

WORLD WAR II JETS

Germany had the first jet fighters in service. One of them, the Messerschmidt Me262, could have dominated the air war, but it was misused by the military. Britain introduced the Gloster Meteor to the war towards the end, but the Me262 and Meteor never fought each other.

HOW JET ENGINES WORK

When you blow up a balloon, the pressure of your breath inside makes the balloon fat and round. You have to hold the mouthpiece tightly or the air will rush out. If you let go, the air rushing out will make the balloon fly away, skittering this way and that.

What is happening inside a balloon is that the air pressure from your breath is pushing outwards in all directions. When you let go of the mouthpiece, there is nothing for it to push against, so it races out the hole. Meanwhile, the air inside is still pushing against the end of the balloon in the opposite direction, and it flies away. And it keeps flying away until all the pressure is used up.

This is known as the third law of motion. The air rushing out the balloon is called ACTION. To every ACTION there is a REACTION in the opposite direction.

Inside a jet engine, something similar is happening. As you can imagine, it takes a little more pressure than your breath to make a jet work! The pressure inside the jet engine is made by mixing kerosene (jet fuel) together with air, then lighting it with a spark. That causes an explosion, which creates tremendous pressure inside the engine. The shape of the engine inside is such that the exploding gas can more easily escape out the rear, and we have ACTION › REACTION.

It's a little more complicated than it sounds, though, because it takes a lot of air to make jet fuel burn. In fact, you would need a room full of air just

MIG 15

KOREAN WAR JETS

Jet fighters proved their value in the Korean War, where most of the aerial combat was between U.S. F-86 Sabres and Russian-built MiG-15's, piloted by Chinese pilots. The F-86's proved to be superior.

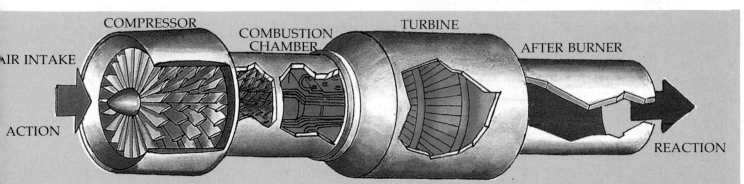

AIR INTAKE · COMPRESSOR · COMBUSTION CHAMBER · TURBINE · AFTER BURNER · ACTION · REACTION

to burn a cup of fuel! It sure takes more than a cup of fuel to make a jet run; in fact, thousands and thousands of pounds of fuel, so you can imagine how many "rooms" of air it takes! How do you suppose we get all that air into a jet engine?

If you guessed that the air is squeezed down so that it is small enough to fit inside the engine, you were right! At the front of a jet engine there is a compressor. It is made like a fan or propeller, only it has many, many blades in rows, and it turns at tremendous speeds. It sucks in huge amounts of air through an intake at the front of the engine and squeezes it to fit inside. Once the airplane is flying, the plane ramming into the air helps the compressor.

After the air is inside, the fuel is sprayed into it through a nozzle, where the two mix together. An ignitor (which is just a spark plug) makes a spark that lights the mixture, causing the fuel to burn. It burns so fast that it is really an explosion. Once the jet engine is started, the spark is no longer needed because the explosion is continuous.

Hey, wait a minute! We forgot to tell you how we get the compressor to turn! That is done by putting a propeller into the burning gases as they rush out the rear of the engine. The rushing gases cause the propeller to turn, just like a windmill. By connecting it to the compressor with a shaft, the propeller and compressor turn together.

The propeller looks similar to the compressor because it has many, many blades. It isn't called a propeller, but a turbine. A type of jet engine is named after it. It's called a turbojet. If you attached a large propeller to the front of the compressor, you could turn it just like the propeller on an ordinary airplane. The engine would then be called a turboprop. Turboprop engines are very efficient at slow speeds and are used sometimes on smaller airplanes or large airplanes like the Lockheed Hercules Transport that have to fly slowly into small airfields.

Some modern jet airplanes, such as the Boeing 747 have engines that are a combination turbojet and turboprop. These are called turbofans or fanjets. Instead of a three - or four-bladed propeller in the front such as on a propeller-driven airplane, a fan with many blades is attached to the compressor.

This fan is located inside a duct that surrounds the turbojet engine. It blows air through the duct, producing ACTION, which combined with the ACTION from the jet exhaust, produces a REACTION.

H.S. HARRIER

DE HAVILLAND COMET

PRESENT DAY FIGHTERS

Some of the best fighters today are the McDonnell-Douglas F-18 Hornet, the British Harrier Jump Jet and the Russian Foxbat.

AIRLINERS

The first jet airliner was the British deHavilland Comet l, which first flew in July, 1949. Just two weeks later, the Avro Canada C-102 Jetliner made its maiden flight.

Today, jet airliners are common. Some of the more successful are the Lockheed L1011, Douglas DC-10, Boeing 747 and Airbus A300.

GLOSSARY

AILERON -Section at the rear of the end of the wing that moves up and down to bank an airplane. An aileron on one wing moves up while the other moves down and vice versa.

AIRFOIL -Shape of a wing when viewed from one end or if a slice was cut through it.

AIR SPEED -Speed of an airplane with respect to the air.

ALTIMETER -An instrument in an airplane that measures its height above sea level.

AMPHIBIAN -An airplane that can land or take off on water or land.

ANGLE OF ATTACK -The angle a wing makes with respect to the direction of its travel through the air.

ASPECT RATIO -The area of a wing divided by the square of its width (or chord). A long, narrow wing is said to have a high aspect ratio, A short, stubby wing is said to have a low aspect ratio.

AUTOROTATION -A tailspin.

AVIONICS -The electronic, radio, and other instruments on board an airplane used for navigation and communications.

BANK - The action a plane makes when it tilts its wings or rotates on its longitudinal axis.

BATTENS -Stiffeners in the fabric of a hang glider sail.

BIPLANE -An airplane with two sets of wings, one above the other.

CLOUD STREETS -Rows of puffy (cumulus) clouds, created by rising hot air.

COMPRESSOR -A device which squeezes air into a smaller volume. On a jet engine, it is a series of rotating fan blades at the front of the engine.

CONTROL WHEEL -A wheel in the pilot's seat to control the airplane in pitch or bank or a combination of the two.

CUMULUS CLOUDS -Puffy clouds that are formed by rising air.

DRAG -Resistance to forward motion of an airplane, caused by the friction of air on its surfaces.

ELEVATOR -Horizontal tail component of an airplane that moves up or down to change the pitch of the airplane about its horizontal axis.

EMPENNAGE -Tail group of an airplane, consisting of fin, rudder, horizontal stabilizer and elevator.

FANJET -A turbojet that has a ducted fan which bypasses air from the compressor of a jet engine to add thrust. A Bypass jet or Turbofan.

FLAP -A portion of the rear of a wing that can be lowered to increase lift and increase drag.

FLOAT PLANE -An airplane with one or more floats or pontoons slung below the airplane for the purpose of landing and taking off from water.

FLYING BOAT -An airplane that uses its fuselage as a hull for landing and taking off from water.

FORMULA 1 RACER -A small, monoplane racing airplane with engine power limited to about 100 HP.

FUSELAGE -The main body of an airplane to which the wings and tail are attached.

GLIDER -An airplane that relies on gravity to fly; an airplane with no engine.

GLIDE RATIO -The distance a glider travels in still air divided by the altitude it loses in traveling that distance.

GROUND SPEED -The speed at which an airplane travels over the ground.

HANG GLIDER - A foot-launched glider in which the pilot hangs from a strap.

HELICOPTER - An aircraft that obtains its lift from a rotor.

LOMCEVAK - An aerobatic maneuver in which the aircraft tumbles in an apparent uncontrolled fashion.

LUFTWAFFE - The German Air Force.

MICROLIGHT - A very light airplane. An Ultralight Airplane.

MONOPLANE - An airplane with one set of wings.

ORNITHOPTER - An airplane that propels itself and flies by flapping its wings like a bird.

PRIMARY FEATHERS - The long feathers at the ends of the wings of birds.

PRIMARY GLIDER - Usually refers to World War II training gliders. The fuselages were open trusses, where the pilot often sat on a simple platform seat.

PONTOONS - Floats on an airplane for landing and taking off from water.

REFLEX - The shape of an airfoil that has the trailing edge turned up, such as on hang gliders and flying wings.

ROGALLO WING - A triangular-shaped flexible wing designed by Francis Rogallo. Early hang gliders were called Rogallos.

ROLL - The action of banking an airplane. An aerobatic maneuver in which an airplane rolls about its longitudinal axis or an axis that is parallel to its longitudinal axis.

RUDDER - A vertical control surface at the rear of an airplane to control or cause yawing about its veritcal axis.

RUDDER PEDALS - Pedals inside the cockpit which the pilot pushes to move the rudder.

SAILPLANE - A glider of high performance that is used for soaring on updrafts of air.

SIDESLIP - The action an airplane makes when it is banked and the rudder is used to prevent it from turning, so that it slips sideways through the air.

SKID - The action an airplane makes when it is yawed with the rudder.

SLAT - A section of the front of a wing that is swung out to increase curvature of the top of the wing, thus increasing lift.

SNAP ROLL - A violent rolling maneuver, where one wing is suddenly stalled, causing the airplane to spin quickly in the direction in which it is flying.

SPOILER - A section on top of a wing that is raised to disturb the airflow and so reduce lift.

STALL - The point at which a wing loses sufficient lift to continue flying, usually resulting in a sudden pitching down of the nose of the airplane.

STICK - Sometimes called the joystick. It is used instead of a control wheel to control pitching and banking of an airplane.

TAILSPIN - A vertical descending condition in which an airplane spins downwards towards the ground. The spinning is caused by one wing being stalled while the other continues to provide lift. Also known as autorotation.

THERMAL - A column of rising air caused by heating of the ground by the sun, which in turn heats the air immediately ____ air becomes hotter than the sur____ gets lighter.

THRUST - The force require____ to overcome its drag so that it can be moved forward. Gliders use gravity . Airplanes use engines with propellers or jets.

TRIPLANE - An airplane with three sets of wings, one above the other.

TURBINE - A propeller or fan that is turned by moving gasses, such as the exhaust gasses from a jet engine.

TURBOFAN -A jet engine that has a ducted fan driven by its turbine. Also known as a fanjet or a high bypass jet engine. Both the ducted fan and the jet provide the thrust for the airplane.

TURBOJET -A jet engine that has its compressor driven by a turbine.

TURBOPROP -A jet engine that has a propeller driven by its turbine, with the propeller providing the principle means of thrust for the airplane.

ULTRALIGHT -A very light airplane. A microlight.

UNLIMITED RACERS -Piston-engined racing airplanes for which there is no restriction of the size of the engine.

WING WARPING -A method in controlling the banking of an airplane - one wing is twisted upwards to increase its angle of attack and lift, and the other is twisted downwards to decrease its angle of attack.

WINGTIP VORTICES -Spinning columns of air streaming from the wingtips of airplanes.

YAW -The action an airplane makes when its rudder is deflected and the airplane turns about its vertical axis.